B & M Potterycrafts.

Project Book.

The Rollifolk.

Introducing Our new Range of Easy to make Figures. The Rollifolk.

Features two detailed starter projects and six supporting worksheets for self expression.

Addendum, variation on a theme.

Design your own Rollifolk challenge included.

1

B & M Potterycrafts

Rollifolk the Egg people.

Contents.

Introduction. The Rollifolk.

Make the body.

Make and fit the feet.

Make and fit the arms.

Decoration techniques.

Hats, worksheets.

Two detailed projects.

Six more projects with worksheets.

Addendum, variations on a theme.

Rollifolk, the Egg People.

Introduction.

This project book sets out to introduce students to a range of imaginary clay figures identified as "**Rollifolk**", so called because the basic shape of each model is a hand rolled egg shape, and also incorporating our family name "**Rollins**."

Follow up books planned are ;- "**Rollimals**" and "**Rollignomes**".

We will outline the basic building blocks and techniques needed to produce these figures and demonstrate how they can be personalised.

Included in the projects are worksheets with weights and dimensions guiding you to build the figures to the correct scale.

We demonstrate the techniques of completing the design by adding accessories such as hats, drawing clothes on the clay, plus features and hair on the figures.

Our previous books have been arranged in groups of stand-alone projects, however with the basic shape of each **Rollifolk** person being the same "egg shape" and to avoid repetition we have changed the format.

We have arranged this project book into sequential sections of common activity with separate work sections for each figure.

Students will decide which model to create, work through the initial sections to create the body, feet and arms then follow the worksheet for that particular model.

Two detailed projects are included which if worked through will give the student sufficient knowledge and confidence to make the other models from the worksheets and use the first chapters of the book as reference to make bodies, arms and feet, and to decorate the models using the techniques outlined.

There is scope in all our projects for self expression and we are sure that after using the projects for a while students will be skilled enough to apply our basic guidelines, create variations on the worksheets and design and make a library of their own models.

That is for the future, meanwhile make the figures suggested and **enjoy your clay modelling.**

Preparation.

A copy of the worksheet will be needed at each clay modelling session.

It is better not to use the sheet in the project book which will soon mark and deteriorate if clay is measured against it.

Copy as many worksheets as you need I normally follow the rule of:- one for an individual, and one per group of four if in a classroom.

To protect the sheets and to make them into a re-useable resource they can be laminated or placed in punched pockets for later storage.

Clay can be pre weighed and bagged (plastic bags with the tops twisted) to keep it moist and to save lesson time or weighed as a learning aid as part of the session if wished.

Clay Modelling Tools.

All the tools can be bought in craft or hobby shops or you can produce cheap alternatives which are just as good and in some cases better and more suitable for use in schools.

Modelling tools shown are the simple tools needed for sculpting small models, most thumb pots and most coil pots.

The paint brush is chosen for its stiff bristles which allow you to rough up the clay to help with cross hatching or obviate the need for cross hatching in some circumstances.

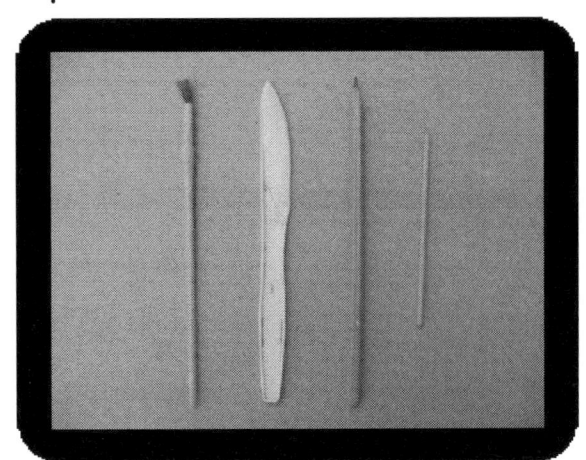

Plastic knives with the serrated edges trimmed using scissors and sharpened on sand paper are a cheap alternative to a potter's fettling knife and more suitable for use by young children. They are used primarily for cutting lengths of clay but can be used as a spatula to smooth joints between pieces of clay.

Pencils or pointed sticks, shown in the picture, are used for adding details such as eyes or hair to models or drawing patterns and designs on pots of all descriptions. The pointed stick shown was made from 3mm thick skewers used in cooking Kebabs. Cut the skewer to the length you need, I got three from one skewer, sharpen one end and round off the other end using sand paper.

The work surface shown is made from 4mm thick, three ply or MDF sheet and is 20cm x30cm. Or can be 20cmx15cm for smaller models..These tools represent a one off purchase as a central resource for a school to be used by any class as required.

Rollifolks, The Egg People.
Make the Body.

In this section we follow a step by step clay modelling process to make the body.

Prepare the clay.

Roll a smooth ball.

Make an egg shape.

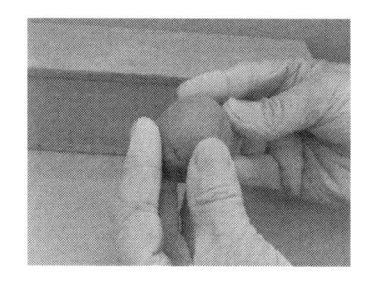

Form the top of the egg

Make the body.

Take the rough clay between the palms of your hand and roll the clay round and round to make it smooth.

It helps if you cup both hands a little and roll the clay around the cup, and as we are aiming for a ball shape cupping the hands forces the ball into the final shape.

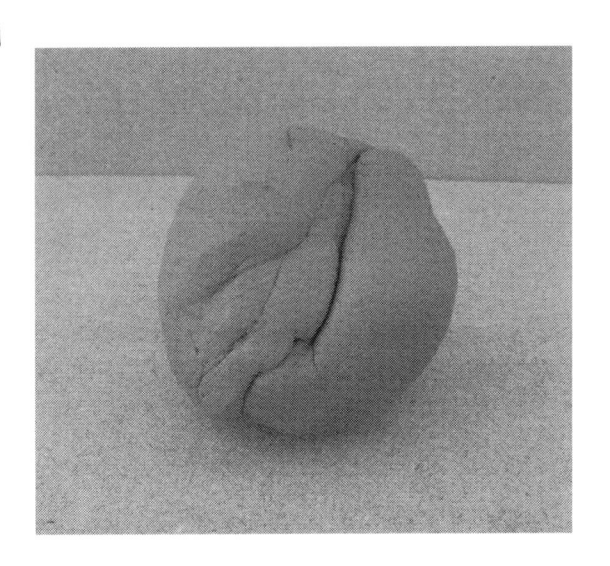

At first apply sufficient pressure to the clay to take off all the rough edges and to remove all the bumps and lumps. Having made the clay almost smooth the next job is to remove any cracks or creases by smoothing them out of the clay with pressure from your finger.

When all the cracks are cleared complete the process by a final session of rolling between the palms of your hands .

This first part of forming the body prepares the clay for the next part in which we need to make the characteristic egg shape common to all the **Rollifolk.**

As we work through the various models presented in this project book you will find that there are three basic egg shapes used to produce the models. I have described them as :-

1. Egg shape with a fat bottom.

2 Egg shape with a fat top.

3. Regular egg shape.

Rolling these shapes starts by taking the ball of clay between the palms of your hands and rolling it backwards and forwards across the palms with sufficient pressure to form the clay into the shape that you want.

First form a short fat sausage shape and then for the first two shapes concentrate the rolling pressure at one end of the sausage to make that end slightly pointed by trapping one end of the sausage shape and rolling it across your palm with the hand at an angle as shown in the picture.

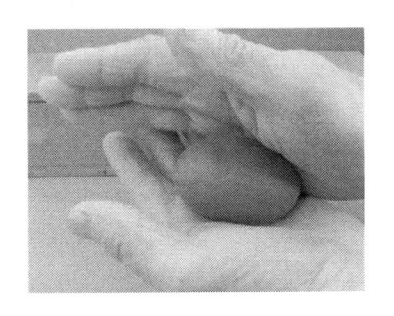

You will find that after you have rolled one end of the sausage shape to make the point the end will probably be creased, use finger pressure to smooth away the crease.

Complete the shape by forming the ends with pressure from your fingers.

Decide which of the two shapes best suits your model and flatten the end you want to form the base by tapping it gently on the work surface until the piece of clay is flat enough to stand upright.

To make the third regular option give equal attention to both ends of the sausage shape to make both ends the same

10

shape, roll one end a little then the other end and repeat this process until you have made the shape required.

Make the body stand upright as you did with the irregular options that is by flattening one end gently on the work surface.

As I stated these are the three basic shapes used to create our **Rollifolk**. There are however many variations possible, you can create tall thin **Rollifolk** or short dumpy **Rollifolk** they are a very varied people and ultimately your creations.

The Rollifolk.

Make and fit the feet.

In this section we discuss the preparation and fitting of the feet.

Prepare the feet.

Crosshatch and fit the feet.

Make and fit the feet.

First roll the clay into a round smooth ball and then into a short jellybean shape measured against the template on the **worksheet**.

When you are satisfied with the length of the clay make a mark across the centre of the jellybean and when you are satisfied that the mark is central cut the clay into two equal pieces to form the feet of your model.

Making a secure mechanical joint in clay the following techniques are employed.

The method of forming the joint is called **"crosshatching"** which involves scoring two small patches on the body with the point of your knife where the feet are to be fitted then crosshatching each foot on the surface where it is cut.

13

To effect the joint we now create some material called **"slip"** which is a mixture of clay and water.

Creating slip in situ, ie directly on the joint is done by rubbing each crosshatched surface with water loaded on the stiff brush until the clay surface turns sticky and is a slightly lighter colour.

Create two patches of slip near the lower end of the model by rubbing the water filled brush firmly round and round on the body.

Repeat this process on each of the feet using the flat surface created when you cut the clay.

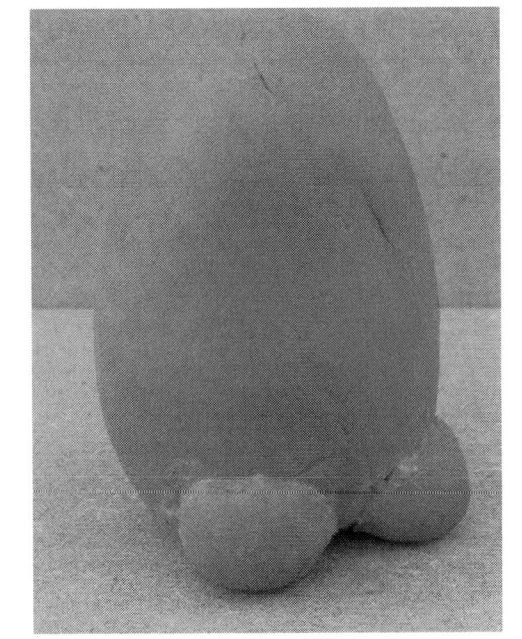

To fit the feet press each one onto the body firmly and with a slight rocking movement.

It is by applying pressure to clay that a firm bond is created.

Strengthen the bond by using finger pressure under the model across the joints.

Rollifolks feet are quite big which helps to stabilise the models.

The Rollifolk.

Make and fit the arms.

In this section we will prepare the clay, mark and cut it to make then fit the arms to our figure.

Prepare and mark the clay.

Cut the clay and fit the arms.

Make and fit the arms.

The piece of clay to be used in making the arms should first be rolled into a ball in the palms of your hands using enough pressure to create the ball shape.

Your next action is to roll the ball between your palms, this time across the palms to form a short sausage shape measured against the template on your **worksheet.** Slightly squash the sausage shape with your thumb which makes it into a rounded rectangular shape.

When you are satisfied with the length of the clay use the plastic knife to mark a line diagonally across the centre of the rectangular shape. Check that the line is in the centre and when you are satisfied that the mark is central cut the rectangle cleanly across the middle to form the two arms of your model.

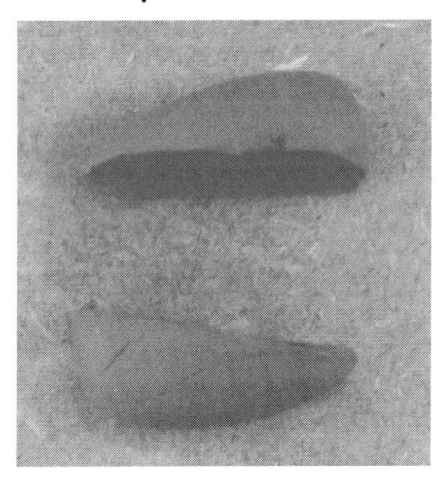

Fitting the arms to the body again involves the creation of slip however this time we do not need to crosshatch the pieces, this is because the arms are what I class as non structural and have a large surface area in contact with the body, enough to form a firm bond.

Create slip using the stiff brush and water on each side of the body in the places where the arms are to be fitted.

Also make slip on the flat areas of the arms where the clay was cut.

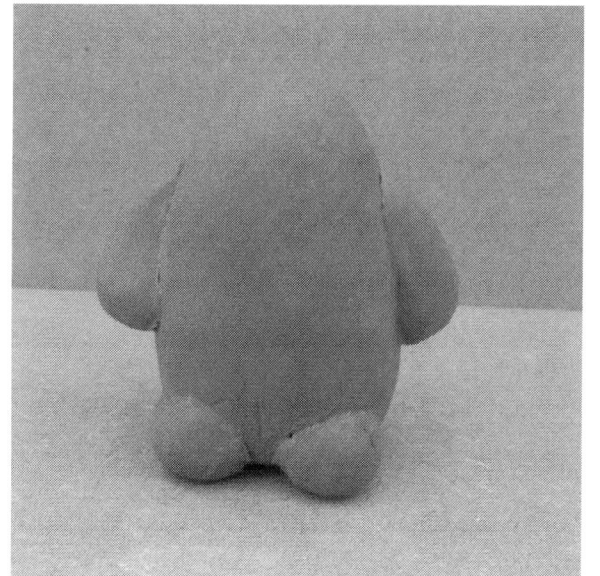

Finally press each arm firmly onto the body and smooth around the joints with your finger tips to strengthen the bond. Give a little shape to the arms by bending them slightly as shown in the picture.

The Rollifolk.

Decoration Techniques.

This section demonstrates the equipment and techniques used in marking clay models to create individual characters.

Equipment and tools.

Techniques.

<u>Decoration.</u>

Eyes and ears.

Noses.

Hair.

Decoration Techniques.

In this section we set out to teach students how to define features and clothes on their models allowing them to define what the model represents by making clear marks on clay using simple implements.

The simple implements or tools are pencils, pointed wooden sticks(prodders) and the edge/point of a plastic knife, **see the section on Tools for details.**

The ability to draw "Fine Lines" on clay is our objective so that you clearly define any details you wish to display on your models.

Pencils and prodders are the easiest to use and we will describe their use first.

Both need to have a reasonable point, the thicker the point the thicker your line will be so look after the points.

Before working on a figure you will benefit from practice on a clay slab with a smooth surface. Spend some time practicing the techniques described, you can use and reuse the slab of clay until you are satisfied with your skills.

Best results, by which I mean the clearest lines, are made by holding the tool between the fingers, not in a writing style but in a manner to allow you to place the point almost flat on the clay with the edge of the point just resting on the clay as demonstrated on the picture. Slide the point along in the direction of the required line.

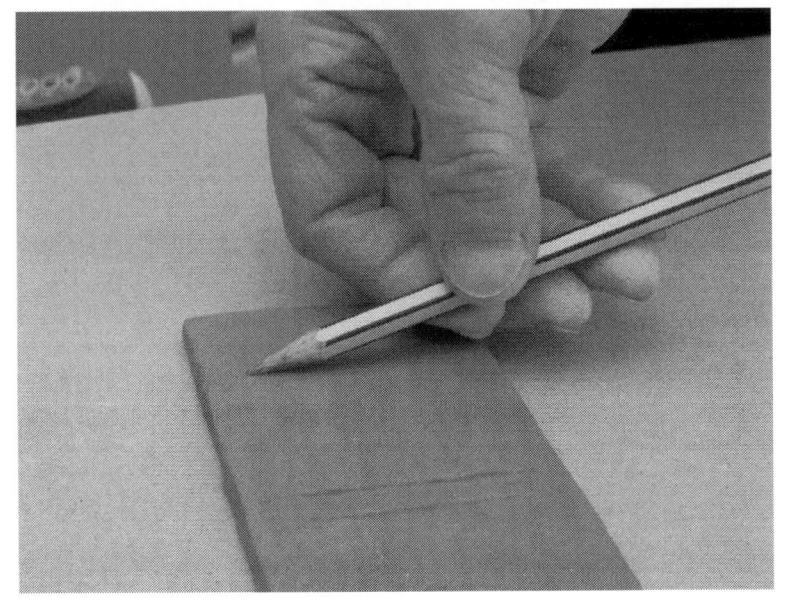

This technique makes smooth, clear lines whereas the normal writing grip can pluck up pieces of clay in front of the point like a plough, this means regular cleaning of clay from the point is needed, and the line created is untidy and not very clear. The other inherent problem is a tendency to dig the point deep into the clay which starts to look messy.

The prodder is also used for making holes to represent eyes with the pointed end and spots and dots with the rounded end as shown in the figure of the caveman later in this section.

This picture shows the results of a small comparison test on the three tools on a smooth slab of clay.

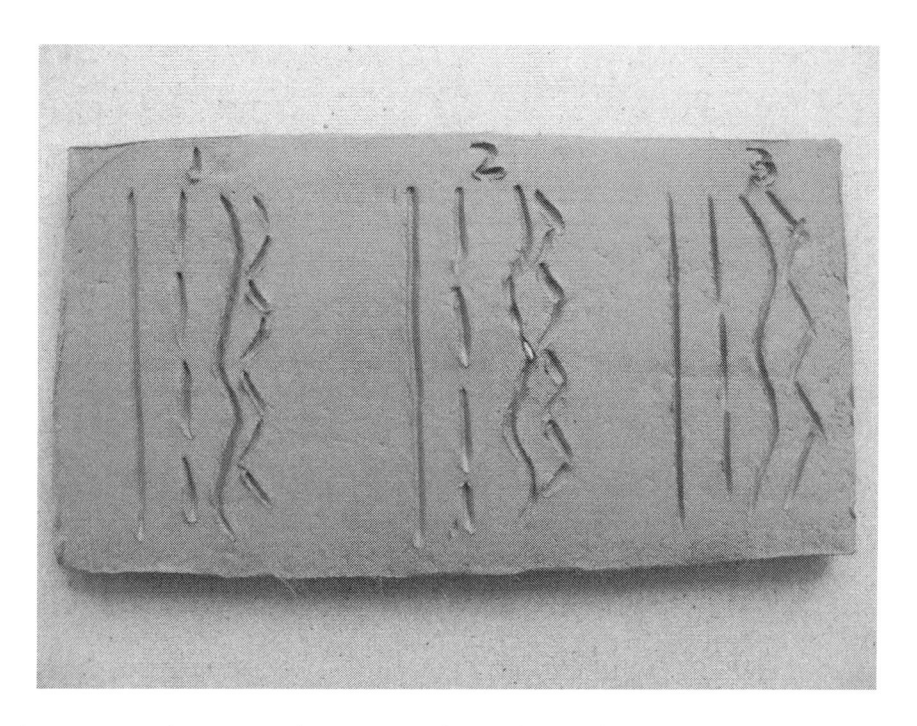

Number 1. Shows the results for the prodder,

Number 2. Shows the results for the pencil and

Number 3. The results for the knife point.

In each case the two left hand lines with each tool are the cleanest having used the prodder and pencil laid flat as shown above and the slim blade of the knife always gives smooth lines if it is used in the direction of the line.

The wavy lines and the zigzag lines were made using the pencil grip in each case, and as you can see the prodder and the pencil both raised the clay at each side of the lines. Whereas the knife invariably makes clean lines.

Drawing clean lines with the point/edge of the plastic knife poses different problems, the blade must be kept upright with the point presented to the clay surface along the direction of the line that you are drawing.

If the point is presented side-on to the clay it will scrape clay from the surface and not draw a line at all.

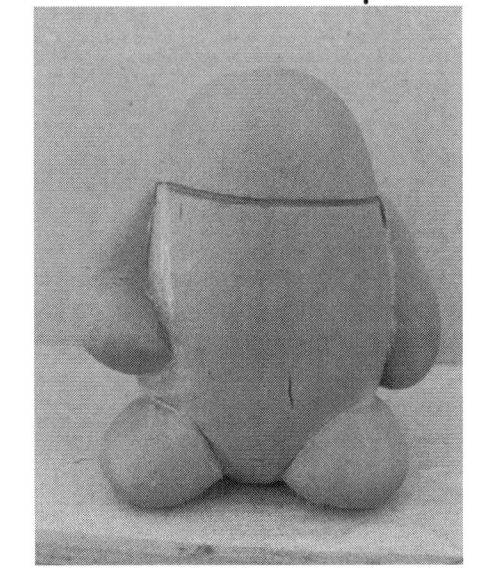

When designing or decorating your model most of the work is done holding the model lightly in one hand with the knife held like a pencil in the other hand.

Lines around the body such as those outlining the neck or waist can be drawn in one movement by placing the knife point in the clay and rotating the body in the other hand, keep the knife vertical to the clay and draw the line that you need all around the body.

Shorter lines can be made using the same techniques with the clay in the hand or supported with the hand while resting the model on the work surface.

Shorter detail marks such as the collar, bow tie or lapels are made by pressing the point/edge of the knife blade gently into the clay surface along the direction of the desired line.

Eyes and ears.

Eyes can be two simple holes made using the pencil, pointed stick or the end of your brush.

More complicated eyes are drawn with the pencil point or the edge of the knife.

Eyebrows are added to suit your model.

Ears are drawn on the sides of the head with the pencil or prodder point and can be as simple as a "c" on each side.

Noses.

Noses on these models can be a simple ball shaped piece of clay attached with slip to the centre of the model's face.

Other options are a small triangle of clay or a carrot shaped piece. If you decide on the carrot shape do not make it too thin as it will probably snap off once the clay is dry.

As I said we generally choose the small round ball as being the most suitable nose for these figures but by all means experiment with a variety of shapes.

Hair.

Demonstrated in the picture are three ways to define heads of hair and the caveman picture shows a simple beard.

The central figure suggests short spiky hair or a shaved head and it was done using the pointed end of the prodder, a pencil point would create the same effect.

The figure on the left side of the picture has long hair combed down the sides of the head without a parting and the third figure has a classical short back and sides style with a neat parting. These were done using the knife point but a sharp pencil laid flat to the head would produce similar results.

In some cases the point of the prodder or the pencil held in a pencil grip would produce a better effect as the hair would tend to be raised slightly from the head and have more texture.

Experiment with various techniques and create each **Rollifolk** model with a unique style and texture to suit that figure.

The Rollifolk.

Hats, Worksheets.

In this section we demonstrate the preparation and making of several styles of hats and caps to personalise our models.

Worksheet 1.

Peaked hats or caps.

Worksheet 2.

Military Hats.

Two piece hats.

Worksheet 3a.

Bowler hat.

Worksheet 3b.

Top Hat.

Worksheet 3c.

Conical hat.

Hats.

The hats pictured in this section are of two types, in the main they are made and assembled and added to the model's head using slip some more simple ones are a peak at the front with the outline of the hat drawn onto the head.

These peaked caps are made as shown on **worksheet 1** in this section. The more complicated "solid "hats are addressed on **worksheet 2** and most of them are made from two pieces of clay, one piece for the brim and the second piece for the top.

In each case we roll a single piece of clay into a sausage shape and cut off a measured piece sufficient to make the brim with the second piece formed into the top of the hat.

The military style hat is modelled from a single piece.

To ensure that these "solid" hats follow the contour of the heads each one is made slightly hollow under the brim by pressing and smoothing the clay with your finger tips as shown on this picture of the Harry Potter style hat.

The hats shown are a small selection of hats to make and with the techniques demonstrated many more models are possible. Use your imagination and look around for different styles.

Worksheet 1. Peaked hats or caps.

The first of these two examples of peaked hats can be used for sportsmen such as golfers or baseball caps in general.

The second one is taken from a lollipop man in which the ear flaps can be up or down depending on the weather.

Roll the clay into a ball then squash it with your thumb on the work surface, measure the diameter against the template on your worksheet.

Use you knife to cut out a moon shape of a size to suit your model.

Make slip on the model and on the inside edge of the moon shape and press the peak firmly into place. Complete the design by drawing the outline of your hat onto the head.

Clay. 2grams.

2.5 cms diameter

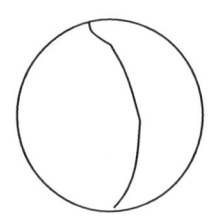

Worksheet 2. Military Hats.

The military style hat is modelled from a single piece of clay.

Start by rolling the clay into a ball shape then fashion the piece into a drum shape as shown in the picture.

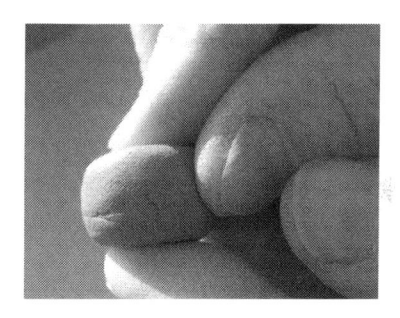

The top of the hat is made by pinching the edge of the clay between finger and thumb as demonstrated, work all the way round until the top is formed. In pinching the clay you may have raised the edge too much, this is easily remedied by placing the top on your work surface and pressing it flat.

The peak of the hat is made using the same pinching technique around one third of the way round the other edge.

Complete the shape by making the inside dish shaped to fit the head.

Clay. 8 grams.

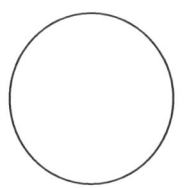

Diameter 2.0.cms

Worksheet 3a. Two piece Hats.

Bowler Hat.

Roll the clay into a ball shape and cut it in half. Roll the two pieces into ball shapes, squash one ball shape in the palm of your hand until it is the same size as the circle template forming the brim of the hat. Throw the other ball shape down onto the work surface which will form the domed top of the hat.

Create slip on both pieces and press them firmly together to form the hat.

With your finger tip press and smooth the underside of the hat into a shallow dish to fit the contour of the head.

Clay. 8grams.

Length 2.5.cms.

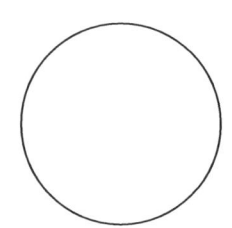

Worksheet 3b. Two piece Hats.

Top Hat.

Roll the clay into a ball shape and then into a sausage shape to the length shown on the template, keeping the clay the same thickness along its length and flatten the ends on the work surface.

Mark the clay at the point shown, one third it's length, and cut the piece cleanly on the mark. Roll the short piece into a ball and squash it on the work surface with your thumb until you make a circle to the diameter shownon the template. This is the hat brim.

The longer piece can now be used for the top of the hat. Make slip on both pieces and press them firmly together.

Make a cup shape under the brim with you finger tip to ensure that the hat fits the contour of the head.

Clay. 8 grams.

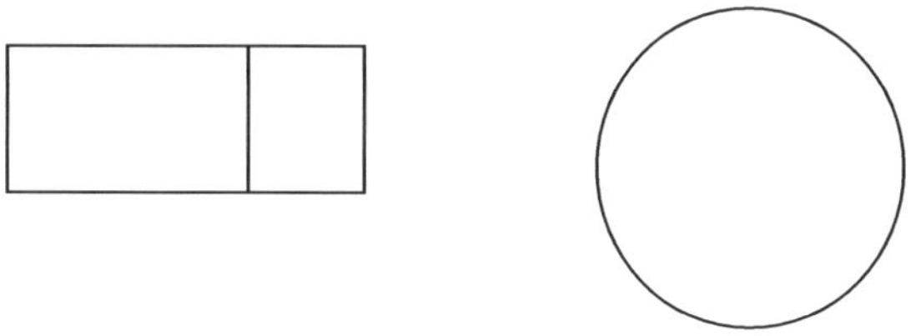

Length 3.cms.

Brim 2.5,cms diameter.

Worksheet 3c. Two piece Hats.

Conical hat. (Top piece will suit the Clown.)

Roll the clay into a ball shape and then into a sausage shape to the length shown on the template, keeping the clay the same thickness along its length and flatten the ends on the work surface.

Mark the clay at the point shown, one third it's length, and cut the piece cleanly on the mark. Roll the short piece into a ball and squash it on the work surface with your thumb until you make a circle to the diameter shownon the template. This is the hat brim.

The longer piece can now be used for the top of the hat by pressing and rolling it between finger and thumb to form the point. Make slip on both pieces and press them firmly together.

Make a cup shape under the brim with you finger tip to ensure that the hat fits the contour of the head.

Clay. 8 grams.

Length 3.cms.

Brim 2.5,cms diameter.

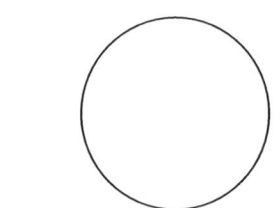

The Rollifolk.

Two Detailed Projects.

This section provides two detailed projects for the student to work through.

Included in each project are complete step by step instructions backed up by still photographs of each stage.

Also provided are worksheets giving the recommended weight of each piece of clay to be used and templates with the recommended dimensions needed to produce the model to the correct scale.

The models are the Headmaster and the caveman.

B&M Potterycrafts.

The Rollifolk Headmaster.

Sequence.

Prepare the clay, roll a ball.

Make an Egg Shape.

Make and fit the feet.

Make and fit the arms.

Add the nose.

Draw the clothes and features.

Make and fit the hat.

Rollifolk Worksheet. Headmaster.

B&M Potterycrafts.2014.All Copyrights Reserved.

Prepare the clay, roll a ball.

Take the rough clay between the palms of your hand and roll the clay round and round to make it smooth.

It helps if you cup both hands a little and roll the clay around the cup, and as we are aiming for a ball shape cupping the hands forces the ball into the final shape.

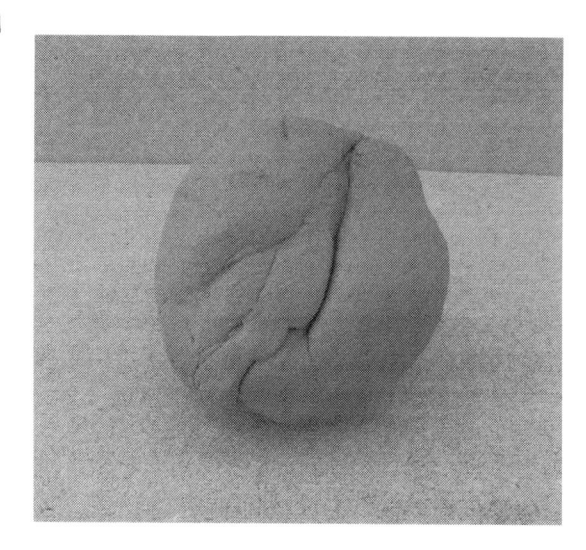

At first apply sufficient pressure to the clay to take off all the rough edges and to remove all the bumps and lumps. Having made the clay almost smooth the next job is to remove any cracks or creases by smoothing them out of the clay with pressure from your finger.

When all the cracks are cleared complete the process by a final session of rolling between the palms of your hands.

This first part of forming the body prepares the clay for the next part in which we need to make the characteristic egg shape common to all the **"Rollifolk"**

Make an egg shape.

Rolling these shapes starts by taking the clay between the palms of your hands and rolling it backwards and forwards across the palms with sufficient pressure to form the clay into the shape that you want.

First form a short fat sausage shape and then concentrate the pressure at one end of the sausage to make that end slightly pointed by trapping one end of the sausage shape and rolling it across your palm with the hand at an angle as shown in the picture.

You will find that after you have rolled one end of the sausage shape to make the point will probably be creased, use finger pressure to smooth away the crease.

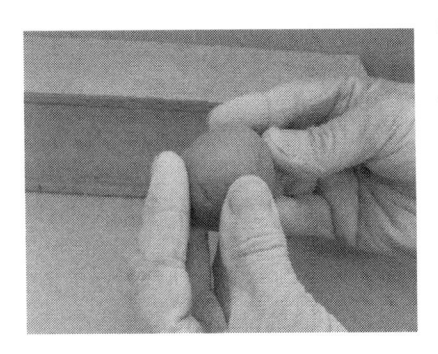

Complete the shape by forming the ends with pressure from your fingers.

Flatten the end you want to form the base by tapping it gently on the work surface until the piece of clay is flat enough to stand upright.

Make and fit the feet.

First roll the clay into a round smooth ball and then into a short jellybean shape measured against the template on the **worksheet**.

When you are satisfied with the length of the clay make a mark across the centre of the jellybean and when you are satisfied that the mark is central cut the clay into two equal pieces to form the feet of your model.

Making a secure mechanical joint in clay the following techniques are employed.

The method of forming the joint is called **"crosshatching"** which involves scoring two small patches on the body with the point of your knife where the feet are fitted then crosshatching each foot on the surface where it is cut.

37

To effect the joint we now create some material called **"slip"** which is a mixture of clay and water.

Creating slip in situ, ie directly on the joint is done by rubbing each crosshatched surface with water loaded on the stiff brush until the clay surface turns sticky and is a slightly lighter colour.

Create two patches of slip near the lower end of the model by rubbing the water filled brush firmly round and round on the body.

Repeat this process on each of the feet using the flat surface created when you cut the clay.

To fit the feet press each one onto the body firmly and with a slight rocking movement, it is by applying pressure clay to clay that a firm bond is created.

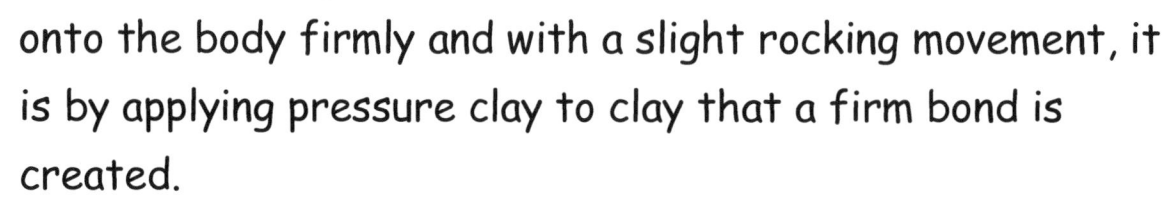

Strengthen the bond by using finger pressure under the model across the joints.

Make and fit the arms.

The piece of clay to be used in making the arms should first be rolled into a ball in the palms of your hands using enough pressure to create the ball shape.

Your next action is to roll the ball between your palms, this time across the palms to form a short sausage shape measured against the template on your **worksheet**. Slightly squash the sausage shape with your thumb which makes a rounded rectangular shape.

When you are satisfied with the length of the clay use the plastic knife to mark a line diagonally across the centre of the rectangular shape. Check that the line is in the centre and when you are satisfied that the mark is central cut the rectangle cleanly across the middle to form the two arms of your model.

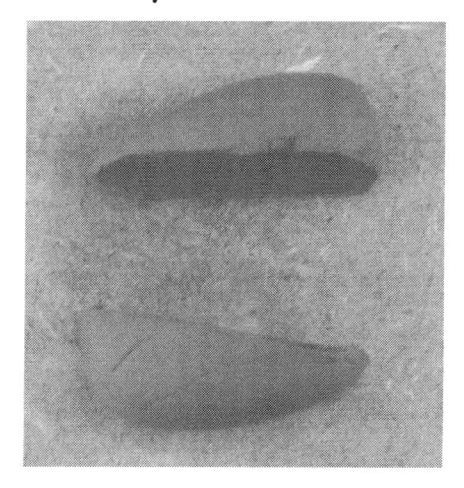

Fitting the arms to the body again involves the creation of slip however this time we do not need to crosshatch the pieces, this is because the arms are what I class as non structural and have a large surface area in contact with the body, enough to form a firm bond.

Create slip using the stiff brush and water on each side of the body in the places where the arms are to be fitted.

Also make slip on the flat areas of the arms where the clay was cut.

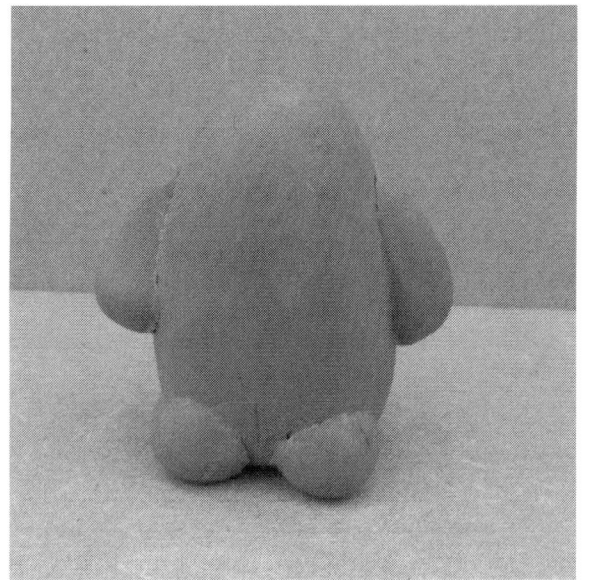

Finally press each arm firmly onto the body and smooth around the joints with your finger tips to strengthen the bond. Give a little shape to the arms by bending them slightly as shown in the picture.

Add the nose.

Rollifolk noses are generally a simple ball shape.

Take a piece of clay of a size to suit your model and roll it into a small ball.

Create a small patch of slip in the centre of the face area and on the ball and press the nose firmly into place.

Draw the clothes and features.

Details of the back and front of the model are shown on the worksheet.

First draw a line with the pencil or knife point round the top of the body, level with the shoulders to represent his collar.

Next add the eyes, ears and mouth with the pointed stick.

With the knife point sketch in some hair, simple straight lines for the fringe and hairline at the back of the head.

His gown goes over each shoulder, drapes down the front of his body and continues below the arms to form a split at the back of the model.

Add a line for the top of his trousers and a line round each arm to outline his cuffs.

Press the point of your knife into the clay to make the collar of his shirt, his tie, thumbs and his pockets.

Trace a line round each boot to make his toecaps.

Finally press the blunt edge, the back, of your knife first between his boots to form his trouser legs then at the back of the model for the back of his trouser legs.

Make and fit the hat.

The hat, called a mortarboard owing to it's shape, is made up of two square pieces of clay.

The fist piece for the top of the hat is 2cm square and the second piece which forms a kind of cup to fit the rounded head is 1.5 cm square.

Roll the clay into a smooth ball and squash it first between the palms of your hands then on the work surface with your thumb, don't make it too thin. Check the size against the templates on the work sheet, try to make the flattened piece just large enough to allow you to cut out the two squares. Cardboard templates could be prepared or measure and cut against a ruler.

Take the smaller square and press it over your thumb or finger to make a cup shape to fit the head. Create slip on the head with brush water and press the cup shape onto the head. Create slip on a spot in the centre of the larger square and press the squares together to form the hat.

Finally create slip on the head and inside the hat and press the hat firmly onto his head.

B & M Potterycrafts.

Rollifolk Worksheet. Harold The Headmaster.

Section 1. Make the body.

Section 2. Make and fit the feet.

Section 3. Make and fit the arms.

Clay.

Body.   100 grams.

Feet.   8 grams.

Arms.   8 grams.

Nose.   Small piece.

Hat. 8 grams.

B&M Potterycrafts.

The Rollifolk Caveman.

Sequence.

Prepare the clay, roll a ball.

Make an Egg Shape.

Make and fit the feet.

Make and fit the arms.

Add the nose.

Draw the clothes and features.

Make and fit the club.

Rollifolk Worksheet. Caveman.

B&M Potterycrafts.2014.All Copyrights Reserved.

Make an egg shape.

Rolling these shapes starts by taking the clay between the palms of your hands and rolling it backwards and forwards across the palms with sufficient pressure to form the clay into the shape that you want.

First form a short fat sausage shape and then concentrate the pressure at one end of the sausage to make that end slightly pointed by trapping one end of the sausage shape and rolling it across your palm with the hand at an angle as shown in the picture.

You will find that after you have rolled one end of the sausage shape to make the point will probably be creased, use finger pressure to smooth away the crease.

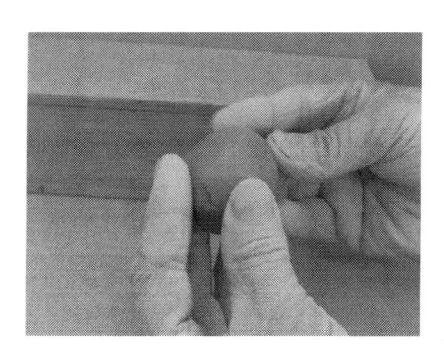

Complete the shape by forming the ends with pressure from your fingers.

Flatten the end you want to form the base by tapping it gently on the work surface until the piece of clay is flat enough to stand upright.

Make and fit the feet.

First roll the clay into a round smooth ball and then into a short jellybean shape measured against the template on the **worksheet**.

When you are satisfied with the length of the clay make a mark across the centre of the jellybean and when you are satisfied that the mark is central cut the clay into two equal pieces to form the feet of your model.

Making a secure mechanical joint in clay the following techniques are employed.

The method of forming the joint is called **"crosshatching"** which involves scoring two small patches on the body with the point of your knife where the feet are fitted then crosshatching each foot on the surface where it is cut.

To effect the joint we now create some material called **"slip"** which is a mixture of clay and water.

Creating slip in situ, ie directly on the joint is done by rubbing each crosshatched surface with water loaded on the stiff brush until the clay surface turns sticky and is a slightly lighter colour.

Create two patches of slip near the lower end of the model by rubbing the water filled brush firmly round and round on the body.

Repeat this process on each of the feet using the flat surface created when you cut the clay.

To fit the feet press each one onto the body firmly and with a slight rocking movement, it is by applying pressure clay to clay that a firm bond is created.

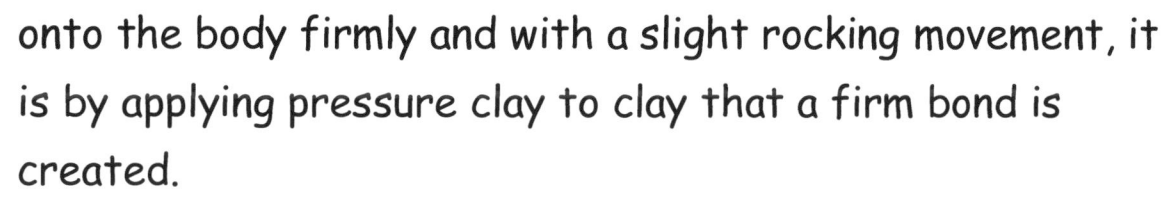

Strengthen the bond by using finger pressure under the model across the joints.

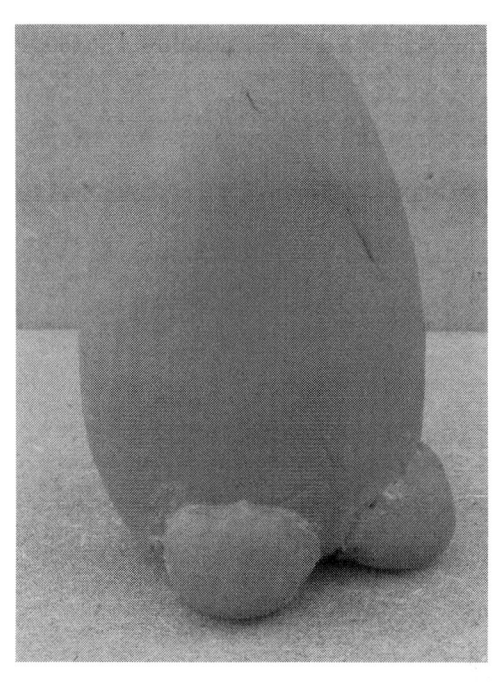

Make and fit the arms.

The piece of clay to be used in making the arms should first be rolled into a ball in the palms of your hands using enough pressure to create the ball shape.

Your next action is to roll the ball between your palms, this time across the palms to form a short sausage shape measured against the template on your **worksheet**. Slightly squash the sausage shape with your thumb which makes a rounded rectangular shape.

When you are satisfied with the length of the clay use the plastic knife to mark a line diagonally across the centre of the rectangular shape. Check that the line is in the centre and when you are satisfied that the mark is central cut the rectangle cleanly across the middle to form the two arms of your model.

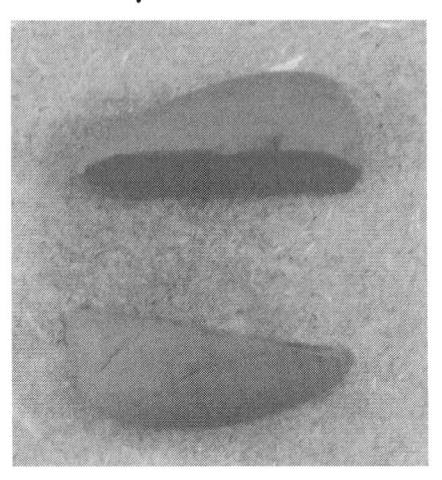

Fitting the arms to the body again involves the creation of slip however this time we do not need to crosshatch the pieces, this is because the arms are what I class as non structural and have a large surface area in contact with the body, enough to form a firm bond.

Make and fit the nose.

Rollifolk noses are usually ball shaped as shown on the picture.

Take a suitably sized piece of clay and roll it into a smooth ball.

Make a patch of slip, using water and brush, in the centre of the face area and on one side of the ball.

Press the nose firmly into place.

Draw the features and clothes.

First make two eyes with the pencil or pointed stick.

To make the mouth as shown on the worksheet use the knife point. Alternatively, to make him shout or sing, push the pointed end of the stick into a spot just under his nose.

Use the knife point to make his beard, moustache and hair.

His skin suit is drawn with the knife point and decorated with spots using the rounded end of the stick.

Make and fit the club.

The caveman's club is made from a single piece of clay and decorated to look like a piece of wood.

First roll the clay into a ball and then into a carrot shape.

This is done by trapping one side of the ball between the edge of the hand held at an angle, and the work surface, (see the picture). Apply pressure and roll the ball across the board until the shape is formed and the club is as long as shown on the worksheet template.

B & M Potterycrafts.

Rollifolk Worksheet. Carl The Caveman.

Section 1. Make the body.

Section 2. Make and fit the feet.

Section 3. Make and fit the arms.

Clay.

Body.   100 grams.

Feet.   8 grams.

Arms.   8 grams.

Nose.   Small piece.

Club.   8 grams.

B&M Potterycrafts.2014.All Copyrights Reserved.

The Rollifolk.

More Projects. Worksheets.

This section provides six additional projects in the form of "worksheets" to work through in which you can apply the knowledge gained in the two detailed projects. Reference can be made to the detailed sections of the manual when needed.

Opera Singer.

Lollipop Lady.

Clown.

Sergeant Major.

Skinhead.

Derby Day.

Rollifolk Worksheet. Opera Singer.

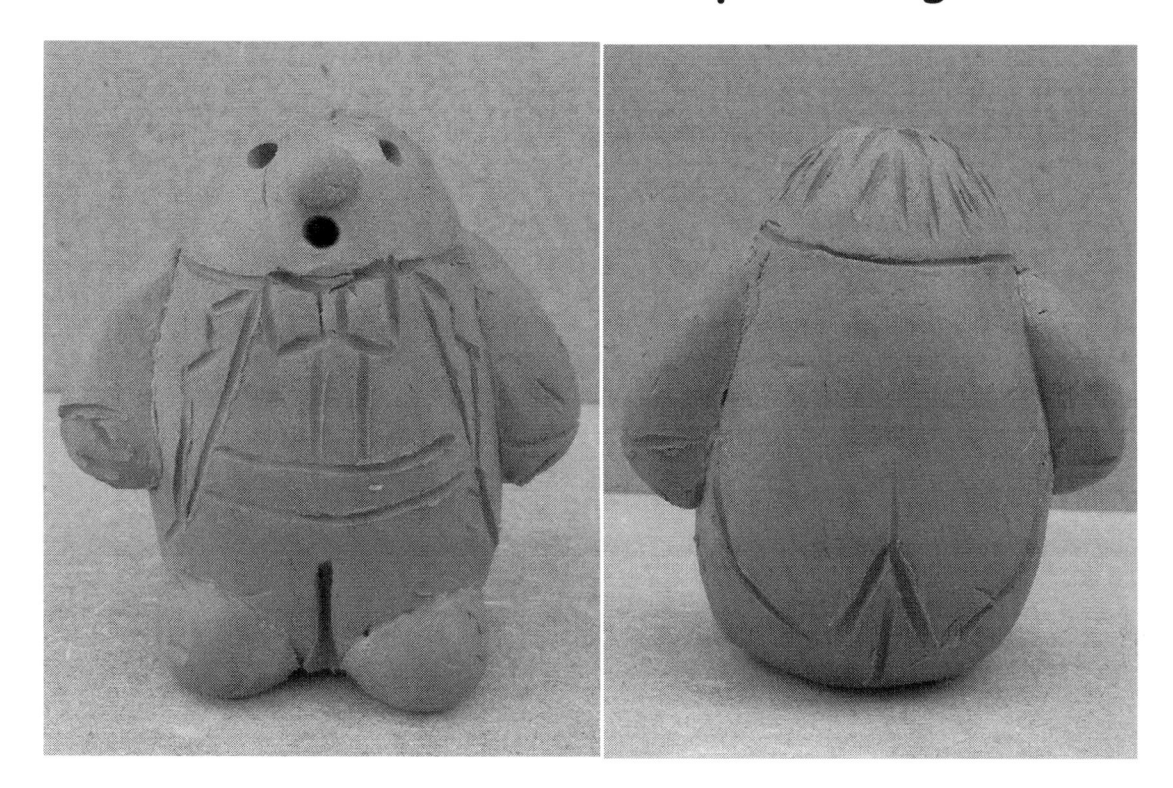

Section 1. Make the body.

Section 2. Make and fit the feet.

Section 3. Make and fit the arms.

Clay.

Body. 100 grams.

Feet.   8 grams.

Arms.   8 grams.

Nose. Small piece.

Rollifolk Worksheet. Lollipop Lady.

Section 1. Make the body.

Section 2. Make and fit the feet.

Section 3. Make and fit the arms.

Clay.

Body.   100 grams.

Feet.   8 grams.

Arms.   8 grams.

Nose.   Small piece.

Hat.   2 grams.   Details in the Hat section. Worksheet 1.

54

Rollifolk Worksheet. Charlie The clown.

Section 1. Make the body.

Section 2. Make and fit the feet.

Section 3. Make and fit the arms.

Clay.

Body.   100 grams.

Feet.   8 grams.

Arms.   8 grams.

Nose.   Small piece.

Hat.   8grams. Details in the Hat section. Worksheet 3c.

Rollifolk Worksheet. Sergeant Major.

Section 1. Make the body.

Section 2. Make and fit the feet.

Section 3. Make and fit the arms.

Clay.

Body.   100 grams.

Feet.   8 grams.

Arms.   8 grams.

Nose.   Small piece.

Hat.   8 grams. Details on "Hats Worksheet 2."

Rollifolk Worksheet Skinhead Sid.

Section 1. Make the body.

Section 2. Make and fit the feet.

Section 3. Make and fit the arms.

Clay.

Body.   100 grams.

Feet.   8 grams.

Arms.   8 grams.

Nose.   Small piece.

Rollifolk Worksheet. Derby Day.

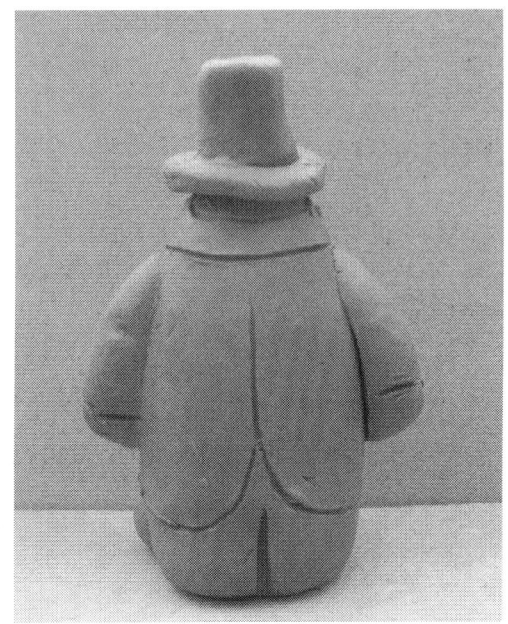

Section 1. Make the body.

Section 2. Make and fit the feet.

Section 3. Make and fit the arms.

Clay.

Body.   100 grams.

Feet.   8 grams.

Arms.   8 grams

Nose.   Small piece.

Hat.   8 grams. Details in Hat section. Worksheet 3b.

B & M Potterycrafts.

Addendum. Variation on a theme.

The variation that I have introduced gives an option to students using the information in this manual to experiment with a different style of arms.

These "new" arms are the style that I have used over the years in scores of figures, so they are a tried and trusted design.

To apply this style to the models simply exchange the diagonally cut arms by using the information on the Sergeant Major worksheet which is part of this addendum.

Apply the extended template and the increase in weight for the arms to keep your models in the correct proportions.

Enjoy your clay modelling. Brian.

B & M Potterycrafts.

Addendum.

Worksheet. Regimental Sergeant Major.

Section 1. Make the body.

Section 2. Make and fit the feet.

Section 3. Make and fit the arms.

Clay.

Body.   100 grams.

Feet.   8 grams.

Arms. 12 grams.   5 cms.

Nose. Small piece.

Hat.   8 grams. Details on "Hats Worksheet 2."

Printed in Great Britain
by Amazon